What My Horse Teaches Me
Insights about life, love, healing, and happiness

Cathy Herbert, Editor

By
Linda Carpenter
Claire Chisolm
Sandy Corriveau
Kim Duckworth
Katie Elkins
Jessica Lea Gadd
Samantha Gothe
Dana Grafft
Valerie Hicks
Tina Lucas
Shelby Lukes
Amanda McKinney
Tammy Mercer
Jodie Palella
Wendy Peterson
Gianna Marie Pickett with Dee Hertig
Elizabeth Pino
Kim Croom Smith
Stacey Stephens
Susan Whitehead
Amy Wiggs
Sandy Wood

Design by Valerie Hicks

i

Cover photo of Kim Croom Smith and Moses Got It Dun:
Copyright © Joe Moliken

Back cover photo of Gianna Marie Pickett and Forrest:
Copyright © Image Hounds

Copyright © 2015 Cherbert Editorial
All rights reserved
ISBN-13: 978-1508997238
ISBN-10: 1508997233

DEDICATION

This book is dedicated to horse owners and horse enthusiasts everywhere who value, learn from, and find joy in life with horses.

ACKNOWLEDGMENTS

I am very grateful to the authors who contributed to this book. Thank you for sharing your experiences and insights.

I also want to thank David Stevens and Roy Baxter, who put the www.Hardknockexperts.com Website together. That site was developed as a portal on which contributors could upload their stories, photographs, and comments. It was an experiment in crowd-sourced publishing that we had previously used in the area of medical education.

You can still add your stories to the Hardknockexperts website. I would love to feature them in future editions of this book.

Plus, there's a new book in progress there: *All About the Dog I Rescued*. Share your stories for inclusion in that future book!

—Cathy Herbert, Editor

TABLE OF CONTENTS

Introduction	vii
A PROMISE, A CLICK, AND A WHOLE NEW WORLD	1
HORSES AND HEALING	7
PEACE FROM PTSD	11
FINDING A WAY	13
GETTING BACK WHAT YOU'VE LOST	19
WHEN DREAMS GO BUST AND THEN COME TRUE	23
MY GREATEST TEACHER	29
AN UNBREAKABLE COMMITMENT	35
NO EXPECTATIONS	39
TRUSTING YOUR GUT, TAKING A CHANCE	43
BRINGING OUT THE BEST IN ME	47
SETTING GOALS AND ACHIEVING RESULTS...WITH HORSES AND IN LIFE	51
WE ALL NEED SECOND CHANCES	57
LEAVING BROOKLYN	63
TRUST, KINDNESS, AND BECOMING MORE	69
THE LIFE-LONG EFFECTS OF LIFE WITH HORSES	73
FOR THE LOVE OF A HORSE	77
A PLACE TO HEAL	81
HOW MY HORSE GOT ME THROUGH MY TEENAGE YEARS	83
A RUNAWAY HORSE, A PRESSURE WASHER, AND A LESSON FOR THE FUTURE	89
THROUGH MY GRANDDAUGHTER'S EYES	91
THINGS ALWAYS GET BETTER--EVENTUALLY	93
LEARNING FROM THE PAIN	95

INTRODUCTION

The idea for this book began to germinate several years ago, as I contemplated the elements of the human-horse connection and why many of us are so dedicated to, and enthralled by, the horses in our care.

I first thought about writing a book describing what I've learned from my life with horses and how that carries over into every aspect of my existence. I put together a sample chapter and a book outline and sent the package off to a publisher with a strong focus on equine publishing. There was interest, but I ended up passing on the project. I wasn't all that enthusiastic about producing pages and pages about my personal experience.

I was a whole lot more interested in what other horsepeople had to say. I'd spent more than 20 years as a writer/editor for equestrian magazines, including *Practical Horseman, Horse & Rider, Performance Horseman, Riding Instructor, Horse Show,* and *the NRHA Reiner*. I'd enjoyed talking to experts and picking their brains about the nuances of training philosophies and techniques. But these individuals, as accomplished as they are, represent a fraction of the horse industry. What about the rest of us? I wanted to know more about the folks who don't train horses for a living, who often spend every extra penny they have for their passion, and who would sooner eat dog food than let anything bad happen to their horses.

For this book, I invited participation of these kinds of riders on a Website, www.hardknockexperts.com, and by personal outreach on Facebook and LinkedIn. Some of the contributors wrote their pieces. Others were more comfortable sharing their stories over the telephone. In those cases, I wrote up the material based on the phone calls and sent drafts to the authors. They clarified or corrected anything that I'd misconstrued. It was a lot of fun. I learned so much about people, horses, writing, and publishing. What more could I ask?

—Cathy Herbert, Editor

What My Horse Teaches Me

*Amanda McKinney and Rocky Top.
Photo courtesy of the author.*

A PROMISE, A CLICK, AND A WHOLE NEW WORLD

By Amanda McKinney

We've all had this experience: You think that what you see in front of you is the whole picture. You're sure you know exactly what's going on and what makes someone tick. When an individual doesn't measure up to your expectations, you are certain that either: 1) they aren't making an effort or 2) they just don't like you. And then you find out that you were just plain wrong—about everything. You'd misjudged the entire situation from beginning to end.

If you're like me, you rarely get the opportunity to take a step back, put aside your certainty, revise your expectations about a person or a situation (or a horse), try again—and get everything you'd hoped for and dreamed about.

That's what happened to me last summer when I adopted Rocky Top, my Tennessee Walking Horse. I had convinced myself—even before I got him—that he was my "dream horse." I just knew he'd become my best friend and companion for life. Instead, I found that Rocky had his own agenda, forged by years of experience in which he'd learned not to trust—let alone like—humans.

Dealing with reality: When dreams don't come true

Rocky taught me a sobering lesson about facing reality. To put it mildly, he was not a "people horse." He wanted nothing to do with me. Even in the close quarters of a round pen, I could not catch him. He seemed determined to get (and stay) as far away from me as he could. Was it me? Did my horse not like me? The whole situation was particularly mysterious because I'd been told that he was "well broke." Eventually, I started to wonder if those words meant something completely different to his previous owners.

I used tried-and-true natural horsemanship techniques to help him learn to "join up" with me. Nothing worked the way it should. For months, I had to use grain as a bribe just to get him into the arena. He refused to focus on me unless I ran him around the pen until he was tired. Only then, when he "gave up," could I get his halter on or saddle him.

Under saddle, getting him to walk or "whoa" was a challenge. Was I doing something wrong? I didn't think so. But when I thought carefully about what I actually knew about him, I realized I had a small clue—he'd been ridden in a severe bit, and his owners told me that he "needed it." At the time, I didn't think too much about it; I was too busy thinking about my dreams.

Can I learn to trust you?

Later, I was glad I'd asked about bits when I got him. It's so easy to assume that words like "broke" mean the same thing to everyone. In retrospect, I wished I'd asked more detailed questions about his routine, what his owners did to get him ready for a ride, what their experience with horses had been, all that stuff that seems so obvious to all of us—but there's no way of telling that the words we're using have the same meaning to those around us (in working with horses and everything else in life).

In the end, I went "back to the basics," spending months to get Rocky to walk quietly. I started trying to trust him. I tried to assume that he would do the right thing, not the wrong thing. It's not that different, really, from working with people. For example, when you interact with someone about whom you've heard a lot of gossip, it's hard to really see the person who is standing in front of you. We tend to bring along all the baggage from past —what we've heard and what we've experienced. I felt that "leaving the past behind" was exactly what I needed to do with this horse.

I also needed to find a way to demonstrate to Rocky that I would trust him. I decided to try a new bit, a very mild Mylers Toklat comfort snaffle. As soon as I put his bridle on, I felt him relax, as if a load of fear had evaporated. When I rode, he seemed to return my trust. Could he become the horse I'd hoped for? Maybe. Walking quietly and stopping on cue were no longer impossible dreams. I believe that he began to enjoy our rides, but I knew that we still weren't friends—yet.

Building new habits

Old habits die hard. Rocky was like a kid who had never learned the basics—when and how to study, when to do homework, when to pay attention, and when to play.

Although his under-saddle work progressed, I still had trouble catching him and often had to free-longe him just to get him haltered. I wondered if he'd ever learned these on-the-ground basics. Perhaps clicker-training might help him understand what I wanted him to do and let him know when he got it right. Although I'm a certified dog trainer, I rarely use this technique (unless clients want to learn it) because my dogs respond so well to verbal cues, encouragement, and reward.

The clicker system worked wonders for Rocky. After just a few days, he was much more interested in me. He seemed happier to be around me. I think that the clicker training introduced something new and, in so doing, broke long-established habits and routine responses. We've all had the experience of watching a small child start to get upset about something, and the problem gets solved by "redirecting" his attention so that he focuses on something else.

I thought of a friend's story about a parent with dementia: Apparently something as simple as refocusing the individual's attention can help ward off episodes of anger and upset. Horses and people—are we really that different?

Long-standing man-made problems: Can they be overcome?

About a week into clicker training, I decided to investigate Rocky's history more thoroughly. He was becoming a nice horse and it seemed that so many of his issues were probably "man-made." He wanted to be a good horse. He just had no idea how to be one.

I called his previous owner. I quickly learned that the man had very little experience with horses. There had been at least five other owners in the last three years. Everyone seemed to have thrown this horse away. I had no way of knowing what his previous 11 years had been.

I reduced my expectations, knowing that Rocky had been through so much. He might never be able to bond with me and be the best friend I wanted him to be. But I decided that was OK.

I made a promise that he would never change hands again. I stepped back and focused on what he needed in order to be happy. I decided that I wasn't going to try to force him into a relationship that he wasn't ready for (now or ever). I would simply accept him for what he was.

Change yourself and see what happens

What happened next amazed me. They say that horses are reflections of our moods, attitudes, emotions, and desires. I believe it. Later that day, I went out to his field. As soon as Rocky saw me coming, halter in hand, he came up to me. I gave him a click and a treat. For the first time, he allowed me to put his halter on without a big production. I gave him another click and a treat.

As I groomed him, we had a different conversation than the ones we'd had before. I told him how sorry I was about everything he had been through. I promised him a forever home, no matter what. I said that I would never sell him. I told him I would still like to ride him, but I acknowledged that he would always be happier out in the pasture with his horse friends. I assured him that I wouldn't keep him separated from them any longer than I had to.

I gave him a couple more clicks and treats after we went through the gate to his field. He stood quietly while I took his halter off—and he followed me as I turned and walked away.

The next morning he gave a whinny of excitement when he saw me. He began to wait for me at the gate. These days, he always greets me with a nicker. If I've been away for a few days, he gives me a happy neigh. He's definitely in my pocket, following me around as I clean up in the pasture, for example. He's always up for anything.

Do we listen?

I find myself wondering if so many of the problems we have with other people aren't similar to those I faced with Rocky. If we emphasize our own needs and bring a long list of wishes and demands to a relationship, we may not be listening to the individuals with whom we want to interact. Until I put my agenda and goals on the back burner, Rocky and I couldn't have a relationship—because it was all about me. Once our relationship took into account his needs and his history, it was a whole different ball game.

Our rides together have gone from disastrous to satisfactory to wonderful. I think about how I gave up on my expectations for Rocky, thinking my dreams would never come true. But, as soon as I did—and saw him for the horse that he was—everything changed. We're friends now, and I believe it's all because of a click and a promise.

What My Horse Teaches Me

*Kim Croom Smith and Moses Got It Dun.
Photo: copyright © Joe Moliken.*

HORSES AND HEALING

By Kim Croom Smith

If I hadn't had a series of life-threatening illnesses in 2003 and 2004, I might never have discovered the healing power of horses. They came into my life only because my husband thought that riding might help me gain strength while I was going through rehab, first for heart failure and then for breast cancer, which necessitated chemotherapy and a double mastectomy. In addition, right in the middle of my physical struggles, I had to deal with the death of my father, to whom I was very close.

By 2005, I looked healthy but I felt exhausted and lifeless, as if all the joy in my world had been wrung out of me. Would horses help? I hadn't ridden in 20 years, but I'd always loved being around them and, well, why not?

The road to recovery, filled with one special horse

We learned of a pretty yellow horse for sale just up the road, owned by a guy that my son always called "Farmer Bill" because he raises border collies and goats. I didn't know that "Farmer Bill" was a very experienced and well-known horseman, Bill Waterman.

I'll never forget my meeting with that yellow horse, Moses Got It Dun. I walked up to him and held out my hand. He reached his neck out toward me and put his face close to mine. I felt his soft breath flow softly over my face. I melted. Every muscle in my tired body relaxed. I felt a peaceful and powerful connection as we looked at each other.

I barely noticed when Bill told me about the horse's ability as a reining competitor and his outstanding pedigree. When he said the word "reining," I thought he must be talking about the weather. We were shocked when Bill told us the price, which I now know was fair for a horse that has been fully trained in the discipline of reining. (Later, I learned that reining is the only "Made in America" sport featured in such competitions as the World Equestrian Games.) But none of this horse's pedigree or training mattered to me: I was convinced he was "the one." After all, this was about physical and emotional healing. What I'd felt when I was around Moses was worth more than the money.

Realizing that I knew nothing, Bill generously agreed to give me lessons. I soon learned how forgiving and patient this horse was. I'm sure most wouldn't have tolerated my beginner mistakes, which were compounded by my need to build strength. My surgeries had left me with very limited flexibility. Heart disease had stripped away my endurance and frequently left me gasping for air. Moses stuck with me. I often felt that he was waiting for me to heal, always demonstrating his kindness. No matter what happened, he never held a grudge.

Learning to live in the moment

The biggest lesson I learned from Moses was about the importance of living in the moment. He helped me to stop anticipating problems and worrying about my inadequacies. I learned to stop criticizing myself for my less-than-perfect body and its limitations.

He helped me to really enjoy—and to build my life around—the many small accomplishments that each day of riding brings, whether they involve performing something as basic as loping for three minutes without being exhausted or as complicated as executing a show-ring maneuver.

That joy of being "in the present" spills over into the rest of my life. Especially after life-threatening illnesses, it's hard to let go of the fear associated with so many things. Activities that I used to take for granted had become accompanied by worries of another trip to the hospital and another rehabilitation process.

Moses helped me to see all that I'd accomplished, all that I could accomplish, and how to celebrate each moment. He brought me through the process of strengthening and healing—and overcoming my body's limitations and my mind's fears.

Eventually my heart improved. When I could ride hard and not be out of air, I knew that I was free at last! Today, I am easier on myself about expectations and goals. I am more ready to forgive and move on. Most of all, I try to breathe love and generosity on those I love—much as Moses did to me on the first day of our time together.

These days, Moses has retired from the show pen and from reining. He worked as a therapy horse until budget cuts put an end to the program. I have to say that when the program director called me to say that they couldn't keep Moses, I was overjoyed. I couldn't wait for him to come home. He joined up with me like old times. But the high point? Going out on a trail ride with Moses and my youngest son. Moses continues to breathe life, joy, and healing into everyone around him.

What My Horse Teaches Me

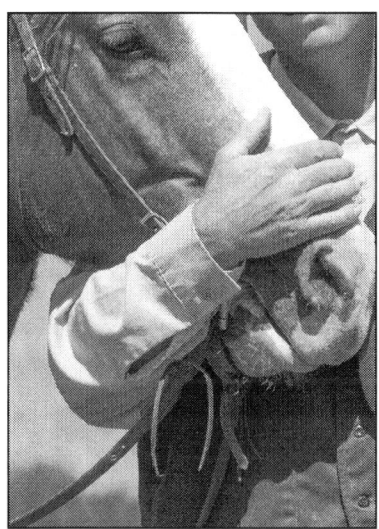

*photo: copyright © BLM Nevada
https://creativecommons.org.*

PEACE FROM PTSD

By Anonymous

Almost 40 years ago, I was diagnosed with PTSD as a result of my Vietnam tour in 1967. My greatest joy is being with my horses and dogs. I have learned through several years of VA therapy that my animals are non-judgmental and I am able to be in the moment when I am with them. They have helped me deal with my PTSD. I feel like a normal person when I am with them. Thank God for my animals.

What My Horse Teaches Me

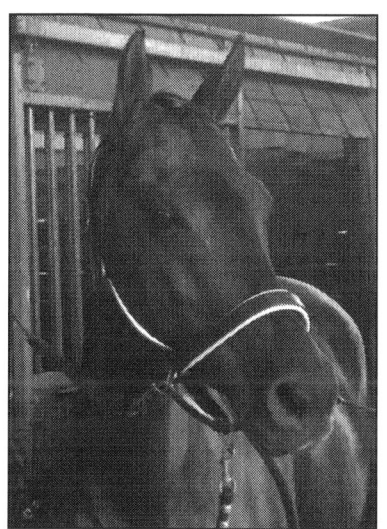

*Elizabeth Pino's "Moey."
Photo courtesy of the author.*

FINDING A WAY

By Elizabeth Pino

I grew up on the north shore of Massachusetts in a small-town non-horse family. My father was an optometrist. My mother loved books and eventually established a used bookstore. Before long, my father joined her in that enterprise. They always encouraged us to try new things, although education always came first.

Never giving up

Throughout my childhood, I was determined to have horses in my life. I started riding lessons at age 4, and I progressed through 4-H. My parents agreed to pay for one lesson a week. To ride more often, I had to figure out a way to earn the money. I became a barn rat, cleaning stalls, doing chores… anything for that extra ride, although my real goal was a horse of my own. I never let up on my parents, often leaving notes to the effect that "If you love me, you'll get me a horse." I may have been a nuisance, but I learned to go after what I wanted. I also learned that "wanting something" had to be accompanied by working hard, trying hard, and keeping at it after too many rejections to count.

I got very creative in my efforts to expand my riding opportunities. My school allowed us to develop extracurricular projects and activities. So I put in a request to work at a barn. It worked: I learned to clean stalls, feed, and ride.

I often look back and think that the lessons we can learn through our involvement with animals aren't as highly valued as they should be. What did I learn? Empathy, hard work, and problem solving. I find it interesting that businesses take their employees to ranches to learn about teamwork, something every child who learns how to ride understands fully.

Today, as a team leader at a large communications company, I use my life with horses every day, as I try to find an approach that works for each team member. It really is no different from trying to figure out the best way to teach a horse a specific movement or task.

Horses constantly talk to you through their movements and body language. It's the same with people: So much communication is nonverbal. Do we listen carefully enough to the humans (or horses or other animals) in our lives? It's a question I always keep in the back of my mind as I try to be more attentive to and more aware of those around me.

A life's journey with horses

I also think about my life with horses as a journey to make my horse (and myself) healthier and happier.

But I do believe that sometimes—as is true with people—a specific horse and rider just may not be the best match. If that horse were a person, she might be someone you'd say "hi" to in the office. But you wouldn't want to go out to dinner or on vacation with her.

That kind of thinking has served me well with horses. I've done a lot of "horse trading" in my efforts to find Moey, a horse that I really enjoy. Along the way, I've discovered that horses, like people, have idiosyncrasies that may affect how horse and rider get along. For example, I had one horse that wasn't particularly responsive going western, with an "I don't want to do this" attitude. But put her in an English saddle, and she was as happy as could be.

My "search for the one" finally led me to Moey—and the sport I do now, western dressage. When I work with her, I try to focus on listening to my horse, on making sure she gets to stretch and exercise in a way that keeps her comfortable. I keep in mind that, in working with horses, it's not "all about me." If I'm not getting the results I want, it's not because my horse doesn't like me. If she's not cooperative, I investigate the possible reasons. For instance, if Moey doesn't want to go forward, I don't automatically treat it as a resistance. I first look to see if something is hurting her. Does my saddle fit right? Is it pinching her anywhere? Is she sore? Usually, I find a reason.

Nurturing, critical for horses and people

A lot of horse training is based on one idea: Make what you want a horse to do the easy choice. Conversely, make what you don't want a horse to do the hard choice. Horses, like people, tend to look for the easiest solution to a problem—but in so many of our horse-and-human or human-and-human interactions, we don't see that connection and how it can help build positive (and nurturing) relationships.

I've made it a point to adapt the techniques that work so well on horses to people. For instance, my team at work handles a lot of software coding. There's a specific process of code development, review, inspection, and finalization. You can't get the steps out of order. At one point, I had a team member who seemed more interested in complaining and interfering with everyone else's work than in following procedures. He would often get the steps out of order and have to redo a lot of his work.

I asked myself: If he were a horse, what would I do? I'd start by separating him from the herd to limit the opportunities for negative interaction. In a horse hierarchy, that might include reducing the likelihood of behaviors such as fighting over food or delivering kicks to establish dominance. In this situation, it meant limiting the amount of chaos he could create for those around him. I found an assignment for him that would, for the moment, minimize his opportunities for interaction with others.

What else would I do with a horse that, say, wouldn't go forward or perform a specific task? I would try to figure out what is wrong. I tried to use a similar logic with my team member. I broke everything down into specific parts, so that there would be no way to skip steps. We had a couple of conversations and "check ins" at key points in the process to ensure the work was being done correctly and reinforce the need to adhere to the established process.

What else was in my toolbox of fixes? I decided to use verbal rewards and encouragement at each step, just as I would with a horse. It worked.

With horses or with people, we need to think about nurturing, in the sense of helping our partners and colleagues do what is needed, happily and willingly. It's a lesson that those of us who work with horses have to think about every day—and we're better people because of it!

What My Horse Teaches Me

What My Horse Teaches Me

Wendy Peterson and Cash.
Photo courtesy of the author.

GETTING BACK WHAT YOU'VE LOST

By Wendy Peterson

I was born with a love for horses. Why? I have no idea. I've been told that I was obsessed with them since the first moments that I could walk and talk.

My first flesh-and-blood horse arrived for my sixth birthday. She was an old quarter horse mare named Julie that my dad purchased for me. The catch? I had to take care of her on my own. Yep, at age 6, I was responsible for another living being.

I was always a daddy's girl, and horses were something we shared that only increased our bond. Daddy was a good 'ole typical show parent, getting up early, out in all types of weather, questioning the coach, etc., as I moved up from 4-H shows to quarter horse shows.

Restoring what was missing

As an adult, I left the horse world to build a life, get married, and have children. Over time, I experienced significant losses that left me off-kilter: My dad died in 2000. A few years later, my husband and I divorced, although we remained very good friends and were both involved in raising our kids. I felt a sadness and a loss because of the changes in my personal life. How could I replace what was missing?

Perhaps because horses had always grounded me and filled my soul, or perhaps because I missed my father, I decided to get back into riding. I discovered that working with horses, and most important, showing my horse gave me the strength, balance, confidence, and the focus I needed in my life at that time.

Showing my horse became an amazing experience. I found that in the three minutes when my horse and I were alone, competing in the show ring, I could quiet my mind. For those few minutes, I could surrender to the present. I had total focus. I was able to make split second decisions and overcome whatever challenges I faced. That small interval of time became the one place where I could completely and truly live in the moment, and I felt like the person I had been and wanted to become again: Strong, determined, and independent. I was complete.

If you believe in a once-in-a-lifetime horse, The Money Train (nicknamed Cash), the horse with whom I shared those moments, was mine. I believe people and animals come into our lives for a reason and when we need them most. Cash quickly became my confidant, helped me to learn the sport of reining, and filled my soul with what had been missing for a very long time. Thanks to his athletic ability and tenacity coupled with my drive and new-found focus, we had amazing success. Cash also brought a calm into my life that I needed desperately. He filled what had been empty and allowed me to become the athlete I am today.

What My Horse Teaches Me

Amy Wiggs' horse Rose. Photo courtesy of the author.

WHEN DREAMS GO BUST AND THEN COME TRUE

By Amy Wiggs

I don't remember the exact date in 2007 when the little filly, just seven months old, stepped off the trailer. I do remember my excitement as the shipper unlatched the rear door. I could hear her pawing anxiously, glad that the trailer's movement had stopped and the breeze signaled a change in the routine of the long trip from Texas to Virginia. She probably wanted to stretch her long legs and run in a field. I waited anxiously.

She was my ultimate dream. The sale ads showed her to be an eye-catching well-bred reining horse that would help my dream take flight, a future National Reining Horse Association (NRHA) Futurity contender who would show well as the highest level and then allow me to compete at local affiliate shows. I had looked for a special filly for a long time, searching through advertisements and evaluating more high-priced elite prospects than I could count. This filly's photographs, full-color in a glossy magazine, were perfection.

When dreams and reality collide

As I watched her back out of the trailer, my dream evaporated. I'd expected her to be as sleek and shiny as she'd been in the photos. She was filthy, as if she'd just been pulled from a mud-filled pasture and thrown on the trailer. The look of pride and possibility that had jumped out at me in the photographs had been left behind at the breeding farm. All of her proportions were wrong, but that could just be a growing phase. Young horses often have "a case of the uglies," like teenagers growing into themselves. All of that would have been minor had it not been for the huge flaw in her conformation that would make any horse person gasp. She was as swaybacked as a 30-year-old nag, long forgotten in someone's back pasture.

Wondering (and hoping) that they'd loaded the wrong horse, I reluctantly took her lead rope and introduced Rose to the perfectly appointed stall in our barn. I called the seller, an internationally recognized "player" in the horse industry. He maintained that the horse was fine. A refund was out of the question. The next call was to my vet, who conferred with others in her practice. On examination, she concluded that my filly had a genetic fault that shows up as a condition called equine lordosis. It is characterized by malformed vertebrae, resulting in a concave—rather than flat—structure of the spine.

Learning the language

Talk about a lesson learned! In the horse world (like so much else in life), hopes and dreams and business can get mixed up. I wanted my dream horse. The people who bred Rose saw her as part of a "foal crop" inventory. Even though we all spoke English, we weren't speaking the same language.

Because Rose was part of their "business," they expected me to see things their way. But I, buying a hope and a dream, expected them to behave differently. I hoped that people focused on dollars and cents would care about my goals for a "once in a lifetime" horse.

How many times have you seen this kind of language barrier in your discussions with your children, your spouse, or your coworkers? Note to self: Understand the language that the other person is speaking as early in the conversation as possible. How might I have proceeded differently? I should have listened to the words they used to describe Rose versus their other foals. I should have asked why some foals were priced differently.

Because I was dealing in hopes and dreams, I had put aside basic business principles. I should have had a pre-purchase exam. I should have flown out to see my prospect and spend time with her before I wrote a check. But previously, I'd had great experiences with wonderful sellers. I had bought my share of horses sight unseen. Plus, I learned that this condition can come on suddenly as a horse matures, so even if I'd seen her in person and she'd looked fine, I might not have had any guarantees—especially if the seller was only interested in a sale and had little concern about whether the horse was or wasn't a good match for me and my goals.

Looking for help and hope

Regardless, I was on my own. I searched for help and hope. Like a parent whose child has a rare and mysterious illness, I posted Rose's story on the Internet and then on Facebook. Had anyone else had a horse with this condition? And shown successfully? What could I expect as an outcome?

The on-line blame game began as I discussed the situation with complete strangers: Was I at fault because I hadn't had a pre-purchase exam? Some people thought I was; others thought the seller was to blame for not disclosing the condition. Did the pictures in the ads represent the horse? The answer to this question was easy: They didn't, but at the time they were taken, they might have.

But things have a way of working out. While I was mulling over what I should have done, I fell in love with this deformed little filly. Exceptionally friendly, she seemed to prefer the company of humans to horses. Walk into the pasture, and she'd be right by your side. Come into the barn and she'd give a "happy to see you" nicker. Sometimes I thought she never took her eyes off of me. I wondered if the other horses had rejected her or picked on her. Regardless, she was not "just another horse."

Changing focus

As time passed, I focused on giving her the pats, scratches, and attention she wanted. I researched her condition. I stepped back from my original goal of a futurity contender and future show horse for me. My questions became more basic. Could she be ridden? What should I do for her? I took things one step at a time. I tried every possible treatment to strengthen her back—chiropractic, physical exercises, massage. I smiled when I thought about the many wonderful qualities of this very kind and willing mare.

I realized that the circumstances I faced with Rose weren't all that different from what we experience in life every day. You start out with big hopes and dreams. Perhaps you want a certain career or a specific lifestyle. You've got a dream all mapped out—except things don't go the way you planned. Or an accident or injury means that everything in your life has to be re-evaluated and re-imagined. I saw life with Rose in those terms, and doing so helped me see everything in my life more clearly—both the things I could change and those I couldn't.

I couldn't change Rose's condition, but I wasn't about to give up on her. So I gave her time in the field to exercise herself and be a horse. I continued her chiropractic and strengthening exercises. I watched her breathtakingly athletic moves as she played in the field. I hoped.

When she was old enough to start training, I called professionals who'd had success with horses in her bloodline. I settled on Francois Gauthier, in Lacuna, North Carolina, whom I later dubbed "The Big Guy." Nervously, I drove her to his farm and led her off the trailer to a new life.

I thought about how sad she'd looked getting off the trailer two years before, and smiled at the contrast. I'd groomed and bathed her. Her coat glistened. She surveyed the farm inquisitively, with the look of a self-confident athlete. The work I'd done had made her defect less pronounced, but her back was still concave.

When dreams do come true

You can imagine my excitement when I received the phone call from The Big Guy to tell me that Rose was going well under saddle. He'd adjusted her saddle pad to ensure a comfortable fit. I drove to his farm to watch her perform. The saddle covered her deformed back. To me, she was poetry in motion. Fluid and graceful, she performed all the show maneuvers with style and finesse.

And, yes, against all odds, Rose did make it to the NRHA Futurity and became the horse of my dreams. She competed against the best horses in the country and held her own. She continues to show and her personality just keeps on shining. She enjoys the company of every human who crosses her path. And me? My dream is still intact. And I love every moment of it.

I learned so much from Rose. The hard lessons: That people have different goals and expectations, and that the business side of the horse world is often only about dollars and cents.

The wonderful lessons: That, even though a dream seems unattainable, it's possible to set the stage to get there through hard work, a clear and honest evaluation of the obstacles (and a strategy to overcome them), and realizing what really is the most important element of your dream.

I learned that my dream wasn't all about futurity competition, prize money, or trophies. It was about bringing out the best in a special filly and allowing her to achieve all that she could.

MY GREATEST TEACHER

By Claire Chisolm

Claire Chisholm and her mare Mie. Photo courtesy of the author.

More than 15 years ago—when I had a completely different life—I heard about a "great deal" on "bargain horses" and started a process that would change my world, leading me away from a reality that was defined by a failed marriage and possible joblessness. (My position as a special education teacher was increasingly at risk as budgets were slashed.) The only bright spots in that old life were my two daughters and my quarter horse mare, with whom I took long trail rides to ease my soul.

When I heard about that "great deal," my first thought was that a horse for my husband might give us something to do together. It might save our marriage. Or perhaps I could interest my kids and spend more time with them. Of course, all of that was wishful thinking. I should have known better than listen to a friend about the "opportunity" to buy two horses and all their tack for $500. I was told that they had to be purchased together and I needed to act fast. They were supposed to be good quiet riding horses, perfect for low-key trail rides.

They were anything but. The large chestnut gelding was so underweight that I could see every bone in his back.

"He's recovering from sand colic," said the owner, as I examined the dirt lot without a hint of grass or hay.

The owner insisted that I try the big horse, whose eyes widened with fright at the approach of the heavy western saddle. The man pulled the girth tight, the horse reared, and fists and curses flew through the air. When the man bridled the horse, I saw scars on the horse's tongue. I may have imagined it, but I thought the gelding looked at me with hope. And before the day was over, I forked over the money, loaded up the horses, and headed home.

Learning patience, building the foundation for a new life

I began to learn the lessons of patience that Harry, as I named the big gelding, would teach me. Every movement, every gesture, every word filled him with terror. I learned to move slowly, with intention, thinking about my goals as I approached him. Did I plan to groom his sides? Brush his mane? Hand him a treat? I planned my movements so that, to Harry, they would be devoid of threat. That "consciousness of movement" helped interest me in the practice of yoga; today, I have my own business as a yoga instructor.

Harry also taught me that there is no "one way" to reach a goal. Under saddle, he was nervous and unpredictable, full of fear. I began to practice yoga in the hopes that it would help me gain more control over my body and become softer and more relaxed in my riding. I needed to be as quiet as possible with my hands and legs. I incorporated breathing exercises into my riding.

The more I worked with Harry, the more I came to see that riding was a partnership based on subtle cues and small hints of communication. I became increasingly aware of his movement, his mood, and the connection between the two. Often, whether riding or working with him on the ground, I felt we were dancing, totally in tune with each other.

Lessons in healing

Once, unforgettably, Harry gave me a glimpse into his past, before colic and malnourishment and beatings. In the pasture, he cantered and trotted in beautiful balanced collected strides, quickly and easily changing the length and rhythm of his stride. He was dancing, performing what I now know to be upper-level dressage movements. And he was happy. He'd come so far in his journey from fear to trust. I realized that he had been teaching me, too. I was learning how to be strong and how to heal myself through yoga.

Soon after, we shared an amazing adventure that proved to me that Harry had finally healed. For reasons I'll never know, he disappeared from his pasture. Perhaps something happened and he jumped out. I've often thought that his former owner, who wanted to buy him back, tried to steal him. The gate was locked and no fences were damaged. But, regardless, Harry was gone.

Moments of trust from a lost horse

It took 36 hours to locate Harry: Neither local officials nor veterinary clinics had information. No neighbors had seen him. Harry had found his way onto the Interstate, running for miles past 14 exits and closing the highway for more than an hour. State and local police and an army of bystanders worked to corner him, catch him, tranquilize him, load him on a trailer, and transport him to a veterinary clinic.

When I arrived, I faced an audience of the more than 20 people who had helped get him loaded.

"How will you ever get him home," someone asked me. I remembered the terrified horse I'd purchased years before and hoped that he could deal with the trauma he'd experienced.

I entered his darkened stall and called his name. He came to me and put his head on my shoulder. With a big breath and a loud sigh, he seemed to whisper "Where have you been, and you won't believe what I've been through!" I cried. I saw the lesson that Harry and I had learned together—the value of trust. Because he had learned to trust me, he was able to leave that place with me.

As we walked to the trailer, I heard the comments from bystanders who believed that he would never get in the trailer. Harry approached the ramp and hesitated. I turned and whispered to him: "If you want to go home, you have to get on." Harry put his head down and quietly loaded without fanfare.

A few months later, I left my life in Louisiana and began another journey of challenges and self-discovery that led to my current home in Pennsylvania. The hardest part was leaving my precious horse behind. But I knew Harry would be safe and happy. He lived out his days as the "Gelding Godfather" to many young Standardbreds raised on "his" farm and owned by a good friend. He never left the farm again.

Harry taught me to trust myself, my instincts, and that we can all find healing.

Years later I attended a special event with a well-known yoga master named Hari. I shared with him what his name meant to me. With profound simplicity, Yogi Hari smiled and nodded his head. "Of course," he told me. "In Sanskrit "Hari" (Harry) means the way to God." And he was.

What My Horse Teaches Me

*Sandy Wood and Rock.
Photo courtesy of the author.*

AN UNBREAKABLE COMMITMENT

By Sandy Wood

Horses represent a connection to my father, a harness driver for 40 years. I spent much of my childhood with him at the track. I raced with him, groomed for him, put all the gear on, and (at least from my perspective) did all the hard work. When I was very young, I was afraid of the turmoil in the paddocks pre- and post-race, but I was so intent on being with my dad that I would do anything and overcome any fear to be with him. Through his world of horses, I learned never to give up and to focus on what I wanted and needed.

After college, I bought an inexpensive off-the-track thoroughbred nicknamed Magic and kept him at my parents' farm. I didn't have him vetted. Soon, I knew that he had problems in his front hooves. He fell on me a couple of times, ultimately breaking my collarbone and leaving an indentation in my skull. Later, I learned that he'd raced hard, with 45 wins on the track and too much wear and tear on his body.

Since riding him would put us both at risk for physical injury, I gave him to a girl who I knew would care for him. I felt horrible about giving him away. Although I knew it was the right choice, deep inside, I believed that I'd given up and abandoned him. When I went to see him a few weeks later, the look in his eye was filled with rage and seemed all too human. He pinned his ears and stood in the corner of his stall, hind leg facing me, as if he'd like to give me a solid kick.

I sympathized: I remembered how I'd felt when dad would leave for weeks on end for a racing circuit. I thought about the sad truth of the harness racing industry. After horses' racing days are over, they often go to the Amish, work hard, and then go to slaughter. I promised myself that if I ever bought another horse, I couldn't allow even the possibility of such an outcome. My commitment to my next horse (if there was one) would have to be for life.

Forging the bond

As time passed, I decided to try again. This time, I insisted on vet checks (I didn't want to repeat my earlier experience). So many horses failed the pre-purchase vet exam. I settled on one horse, Rock. His vet check wasn't perfect, but as my dad would say, "no horse is perfect." I wanted to show in quarter horse events. Rock had the mileage and experience to make it happen, but "there are quirks," said the seller. They were reflected in his price. When I tried him, we clicked. I took the chance.

I discovered that, although Rock is perfect 90% of the time, his so-called "quirks" can make him unpredictable. In a split second, and for no apparent reason, he can go from doing his job to shying in terror and then trembling in fear. My trainer felt he was unsafe for me and was reluctant to coach me unless I got a new horse. I thought of my father and my commitment to Rock. I said "no." I figured I'd manage somehow.

Riding Rock became both a commitment to him and to myself. I'm a devout Christian. I believe that animals have spirits and souls, just as we do. Anyone who purchases a horse should do so for the right reasons—and it's essential to put the horse first, not yourself. This is the same principle that guides my work as an elementary school principal. I put my students first. I don't want to see teachers coming and going. I believe in long-term commitments.

Those beliefs and objectives have formed the basis of my work with Rock. Our relationship is about more than going to a horse show and winning a ribbon (and we've won lots). What's important to me is that our relationship endures through the good times and the tough times.

Overcoming a broken neck

But one incident tested my resolve. Rock suddenly shied. I came off. But this was no ordinary fall: My neck was broken. When I recovered sufficiently to ride, I gathered up all my courage. I thought back to my childhood, my fear of the harness horses, and my love for my dad—and the lesson he taught me to never give up. I faced the challenge. I honored my commitment. It was a good decision.

Rock and I have been together for a long time now. Perhaps because we have become more of a team, the number of shying incidents has decreased. Maybe I'm better at sensing and defusing them.

Or it may be that we understand a little more of what makes each other tick. I'm thinking about how upset I was not long ago when my greyhound passed away. At the barn, I had the feeling that Rock knew that something tragic had happened. Perhaps it's a sign of a connection that we have, that unbreakable bond. On that day—and ever since—he has behaved differently, with more kindness and love. Others have noticed that he is more willing, as if trying to give me comfort.

Sometimes I think that Rock is not in the best of hands with me, that a more skilled rider might be a better match. Then I realize that he could do a whole lot worse. And we get back to business—and a long future together.

NO EXPECTATIONS

By Kim Duckworth

*Kim Duckworth and Mickey.
Photo courtesy of the author.*

Sometimes relationships—in the horse world as in life—just happen. You don't think that someone you meet by chance will turn out to be a friend for life. Or that the little horse you met 10 minutes ago can become the horse of a lifetime. You never imagine that a specific horse will open his heart to you and all you have to do is say "yes." Sometimes, things just happen.

I've never really thought about how remarkable that is until I started reminiscing on how I encountered my little gelding Mickey almost a decade ago. At the time, I'd recently lost my beloved Nifty Bueno to old age. I was searching for a new horse. I had looked at quite a few, but nothing seemed to be a fit for me (although, in telling this story, I have no idea what a "fit" would have been). I can say that as an over-40 single mom on a limited budget, I wanted something safe. I have a long list of injuries from a life spent from breaking, training, and exercising steeplechasers. I told myself that my goal was an all-around, broke, fun horse that my kid and I could share. I wanted something I could just get on and ride.

The bold, the brave, and a perfect match

When I got a call about a little three-year-old reiner, I listened—with no expectations. I went to check him out, as I'd done so many times before. He was a cute little guy, maybe 14.2, a dun quarter horse with a smart eye, sturdy frame, athletic looks, and beautiful movement. The hint of boldness in his eye appealed to me. Much later, I discovered that he was related to my dear old Nifty Bueno.

I got on and away we went. He showed lots of energy and go, although he listened very well. He was quite curious. I wasn't surprised about these qualities: they matched the look in his eye. One of the most endearing things about horses is that they generally tell you exactly what they are, if you take the time to look. He had spent little time out of an enclosed arena setting, so I asked the trainer if I could take him out of the ring and into the woods on a short trail ride.

"We've never done that," the trainer replied. "But it should be OK."

I had no expectations, but I was pleased when I saw that he clearly enjoyed the exploration. With just a bit of coaxing, he even crossed a creek. He was relaxed, curious, and happy to be somewhere new on an adventure. On the way back to the barn, I realized that I'd already made my decision. He was coming home with me.

I still had no expectations, but in our time together, Mickey and I have done trail rides, a hunter pace, and put on a reining demonstration. He gets along great with my little herd. He is wonderful with my eight-year-old daughter. We started jumping this year—with no expectations—and again he is awesome, loving it and never refusing. His kindness and generosity continue to touch my heart.

Sometimes, when I ride him, I think how much he reminds me of my special Nifty Bueno, my "once in a lifetime" horse. I had no expectations when I bought him and have never "demanded" that he fill a specific role—as a hunter, jumper, reiner, or anything else. But he's done everything I've ever asked him to do.

What did I learn from this ongoing adventure? I learned you're never too old to take chances. I learned the importance of an open heart when it comes to everything—and especially when it comes to horses, for they open their hearts to you if you give them a chance. I used to say I had a "once in a lifetime" horse. Now I've had two of them.

What My Horse Teaches Me

What My Horse Teaches Me

TRUSTING YOUR GUT, TAKING A CHANCE

By Tina Lucas

Tina Lucas and Rita. Photo: Copyright © Sara Raiford Photography 2015.

My horse Rita (her registered name is Shake a Senorita) came into my life as a result of a split-second decision based on intuition—and one that profoundly changed my life. She's brought me a wonderful circle of close friends. Thanks to her, I continue to learn new riding skills. But most important, Rita gave me the courage to trust my gut and take a chance.

What set the stage for all these terrific changes in my life? Something that seemed quite simple: I had decided that I wanted to try reining, a very specialized Western equestrian sport based on working cattle. The problem? My horse was an English hunter. My first thought: Perhaps my hunter can learn these new skills. It was, I realized, a long shot. Reiners are bred for the job, with short, stocky builds that enable them to easily perform the complex and demanding maneuvers. The training process often takes two years or more.

Still, I decided that retraining my hunter was worth a try, so off he went to a reining trainer. Over the next few months, I realized that asking my horse to make such a dramatic career shift was the equivalent of trying to put a round peg in a square hole. One day, I simply accepted the fact that it might be time for a new horse for me, and a new owner for my hunter. Within 48 hours, my world changed forever.

A leap of faith to a new world

On the day I had my "ah-ha" moment, quite a few wheels began to turn. A friend told me about a mare she knew that had foaled a few months before. That was Rita. The owners planned to keep the foal but wanted to sell the mare. I got an earful of pedigrees and bloodlines and performance records—which went right over my head. (I have since learned that this is a favorite topic of conversation among reining enthusiasts and can keep an audience enthralled for hours.)

What did I actually hear? She hadn't been shown or ridden in a while, but she was, in financial terms, a good deal. My friends were beyond enthusiastic about her, and the excitement in their voices turned out to be contagious. I bypassed vet checks, took the advice of my friends, and wrote a check. For reasons that I couldn't explain at the time, doing this just felt right. It didn't matter that it was a lot of money, or that my gelding still needed to be sold. Or that I'd be paying boarding and training on two horses within my one-horse budget.

I realized that I'd been struggling with the recent death of my mother. Taking a chance on Rita seemed, somehow, like something mom would want me to do. I almost felt that the mare was a present from my mom to me. I brought Rita home the next day—and got a phone call that my gelding had caught the eye of a buyer who could give him a "forever" home and let him do the activities he liked.

I've often thought about this amazing sequence of events. I was never officially looking to buy a new horse or sell an old one, and all this took place over just 48 hours. It was a total leap of faith. I just believed that Rita was destined to be in my life. I have never experienced one day of regret.

So many opportunities

Rita has opened up my world to so many opportunities. Because of her, I have an extended family of reiners and horse show enthusiasts. Many of these friends come from entirely different walks of life. But for a common bond of reining, I would never have met these wonderful people.

She's helped me master the maneuvers of reining—and she continues to teach me. Trust me, I still have so much to learn. She has a ton of try and heart, and she is patient and forgiving with me, her rookie companion.

She has taught me that nine times out of 10, the problems we encounter are created by me, not her. She does what I ask, and if I ask incorrectly, things don't go so well.

She has given me the courage to go in that pen and show my horse.

She has taught me that great things can come in plain packages. She is neither flashy nor colorful, with no long flowing mane or eye-catching white markings. She's just a solid sorrel mare, but she holds my heart. While she is not perfect, and no horse is, she is perfect for me.

She has earned my trust, as I can only hope I am earning hers. She has taught me that time, patience, and a little try can go far.

And most important, she taught me, sometimes, you have to let your heart control your head. You just gotta take a deep breath—and buy the damn horse!!

*Samantha Gothe and Lucy.
Photo courtesy of the author.*

BRINGING OUT THE BEST IN ME

By Samantha Gothe

It's an old adage filled with so much truth: "Some horses will test you, some will teach you, and some will bring out the best in you."

Lucy (her registered name is Steady Sparkler) is the horse that has brought out the best in me, as a rider and showman, and as a partner. She's taught me about what is possible in the horse-human relationship, and how much joy that can bring.

It's a lesson I've been longing to learn for many years. My childhood revolved around horses. It all began when, in exchange for lessons, I mucked stalls and did chores at a boarding stable. As soon as I was old enough, I got a part-time job and leased a horse. Every dime I made went toward his expenses. I wished for more. I watched the boarders—girls with fancy show horses, all the coaching and private lessons they wanted, and exquisite tack—as they rode and showed highly trained horses. I hoped that, one day, I could ride at their level. I doubted I'd ever get the chance. But I knew that, someday, I'd give it my best shot.

Years later, happily married, with a good job, and still itching to follow my childhood dream, my husband and I decided to investigate the western sport of reining. I didn't know much about the training required for this discipline, but I liked its look and feel. Horses perform on a loose rein, without intimidation. The saddles and bridles have a "working horse" look, without a lot of silver or fancy decorations.

We began to shop for a horse, perusing ads and visiting barns. We saw horses that promised all manner of accomplishments. Most had years of training and show-ring success. They performed reining's signature moves—spins and sliding stops—with ease. But none of them really jumped out at me. What was I looking for? I didn't know.

Finding a quiet connection

And then I saw Lucy, barely saddle-broke as a five year old. I couldn't take my eyes off of her, spellbound by her beautiful dark chestnut color and spotted white blaze. I felt, somehow, that we understood each other. I was surprised that her price was so much lower than that of the other reiners we'd looked at. It didn't occur to me that her price reflected the fact that she was very behind in her training—so far behind that the odds of her ever getting to the show ring were considered to be poor.

Most horses her age had extensive show records. She barely had steering. But she was what I wanted. I wrote the check, and I have never looked back with anything other than happiness that she came into my life.

It surprised everyone (except my husband and me) that Lucy progressed so quickly in her training. She seems to enjoy every minute and every aspect of her job. She always wants to please and never tries to cheat me. I'm trying to be impartial when I say that she is one of the best horses I have ever had the pleasure of sitting on. She always surprises anyone who rides her.

Mentally, she is very quiet and calm—I think that's what I saw initially and what drew me to her so strongly. People often think that a quiet mind goes along with a kind of physical dullness. But that's not Lucy: Ask her to perform, and you'll feel extreme, quick athleticism, fueled by a heart and a desire to please that is hard to come by.

Thus far in my life, she has been the only horse I feel is my true partner. I understand a silent language between us, and she answers every question I ask.

Partners in the show ring

I started showing Lucy two years ago. We made our reining debuts together. Occasionally, I think about the kids from my childhood, with their fancy horses, and I know that I have fulfilled my childhood dream. I do ride at their level, thanks to Lucy.

When we go into the show pen, I feel the connection that I felt when I first saw her, a feeling that we understand each other and that, when I ask her to do something, she will know what I want and give me all she can. That feeling helps me show better, and it keeps her happy. Sometimes, when we're getting ready to show, I think I can almost hear her saying "Yes, let's do this." And I've done so much of the work of training and teaching Lucy on my own. We've grown and learned together.

Perhaps because of this, I feel an even greater connection with her: We trust and rely on each other.

I'm thrilled, and blessed, at the success we've had. But it's not about the winning or the competition for me: What means the most to me is our relationship. The connection is unlike any other, and it brings out the best in me—and in Lucy.

What My Horse Teaches Me

*Commandalena and Dana Grafft.
Photo courtesy of Valerie Hicks.*

SETTING GOALS AND ACHIEVING RESULTS... WITH HORSES AND IN LIFE

By Dana Grafft

I rode a lot as a teenager and young adult before I took a 20-year break to establish a life, family, and career. Two years ago, I re-entered the horse world. When I did, I learned more than I ever imagined possible about goals and focus. These lessons have made (and continue to make) a difference in every aspect of my life. My teacher? A 22-year-old stallion named Commandalena.

Lesson #1: Conquering fears, letting go, and building trust

As a teenager, when I galloped on horseback I felt as if I was flying, free of every worry or care. But when I returned to riding—older, less adventuresome, and more aware of the possibility of injury—going fast was terrifying. This was a problem, since I planned to resume competing in reining, the sport of my childhood. This discipline involves flying full-speed on circles and thundering down—at an ever escalating speed—to the sport's signature maneuver, the sliding stop.

To get a glimpse of that maneuver and why I found it so intimidating, let me explain the mechanics: To start with, you're moving at a pretty good clip of a gallop. Then you head down an arena that may be 300 feet in length and build even more speed. By the time you get to your destination, more than three-fourths down the pen, you definitely feel the wind on your face and wonder if you can possibly go any faster. And you ask your horse for just a bit more speed. Immediately after you feel him accelerate even more, you say "whoa" to ask him to really put on the brakes for a sliding stop, in which he brings his hind legs far under his body and drops his hips, so that he's almost sitting down. He slides (thanks to slick hind shoes with small extensions that work like skis) forward with his hind legs, leaving long lines of deep troughs in the dirt, while he walks forward with his front legs. Seems strange? It's based on the moves required in working cattle. This sport has, in some fashion or another, been around since cowboys held contests to gauge their horses' ability and training.

From the rider's perspective, the horse's big, physical moves come on suddenly. Sometimes, you feel like your saddle has just dropped a foot or more out from under you. Or you worry that his moves might make you lose your balance so that you fly over his head and onto the dirt. You may fear that he will ignore you and run on, out of control.

Getting a good stop requires two things 1) you have to know how to adjust your body position and stay out of your horse's way as he does his job and 2) you have to trust him to do his job. And trust is the hardest component to learn, particularly if you're—like me—one of those driven perfectionists who feels the need to be in control of everything.

I am fortunate in that I have a very experienced horse, the internationally known stallion Commandalena. He was more than willing to do what I asked every time. But I had to learn to trust him to do his job. As is true in every aspect of life, if you're working with someone, you need to function as a team. For instance, you may have to step back and let a coworker do his job, even if the way he does it is a little different from the way you would handle things. Sometimes, you have to adjust your way of working for the benefit of the team.

I had a very hard time translating this knowledge into my rides. Commandalena knew his job very well. But I had trouble allowing him to do it. When I watched videos of my rides, I could see that I continually interfered with him, picking up the reins and asking him to slow when I worried about speed (even after I'd just asked him to go faster). He was confused about whether to slow down or speed up. In business parlance, I saw that I was trying to micromanage each stride and making it impossible for him to do his job.

I decided that the only solution was to set things up so I had to trust my horse 100%. So I took off the bridle and just rode. It was the best decision I ever made. By forcing myself to trust him, I learned that if I did less, he was willing to give me more. That's a lesson I can apply throughout my life!

Lesson #2: Looking ahead, planning for the future, and putting mistakes behind you

I'm a very positive and forward-thinking person. In everything I do, I try to think ahead and plan to the best of my ability, navigating the course as I go. I know that success rarely happens without effort, drive, determination, a positive attitude, and clear goals.

In all of my showing over the past two years, I've learned to look ahead and focus for every fraction of every second.

I know that if I lose focus for just an instant, everything may fall apart. The intensity of this concentration is something I've tried to develop in other aspects of my life and in situations where just a little more concentration can make a good outcome even better.

Here's how it works in the show ring. Each pattern I perform lasts about three minutes. That's the time I have to go big or go home. So, for each instant, I need to concentrate on looking ahead to each maneuver, working through it, and moving on to whatever comes next. That also means putting any mistakes behind me immediately. If, while you're competing (or performing any task), you concentrate on what just happened or what you did wrong the last time you tried to do something—instead of what will happen next—you won't be at your competitive best. You'll tend to second-guess yourself and become indecisive and timid.

Working with my horse to achieve this intense level of focus has allowed me to accomplish more in the last two years than ever I ever expected, and certainly far more than I was able to achieve when I rode horses more than 20 years ago. Here are some of the lessons I learned about setting goals that apply to my life in and out of the show ring. I learned to:

Think clearly about my goals. When I bought my horse two years ago, I had one set of goals, and they changed over time, in response to what I saw and felt as I worked with him. I should add that, when I bought him, he was a 20-year-old stallion, had significant earnings, but had showed very little over the past decade. In spite of all his accomplishments, buyers were unwilling to take a chance on an older horse and his price had been dropped several times. I decided to give it a go, believing what his trainer had told me about his soundness, mind, and ability. He was far more than I had ever hoped for.

My goals, at first, were to show him a little and then breed him to a few mares in the hopes of getting a nice horse for the future. Those goals were quickly reshaped. Before the year was done, we had 45 wins and multiple awards. Other mare owners wanted to breed to my horse.

All year long, I had to keep in mind that goals had to exist within the context of what is realistic and achievable. In this case, I was fortunate. As I re-evaluated my goals, I could expand them. But I would have been as willing—if reality had been different—to have downsized them to something that seemed possible when I took a good, hard look at reality.

Prioritize my goals. I set simple goals for 2014: Show as much as I could and as well as I could, while breeding Commandalena to a few mares. Those goals really didn't change. Still, when we started to win consistently, a lot of people noticed—and began to ask about him as a stallion. And that led me to my 2015 goal of standing him to the public as a breeding stallion.

This year, my goals have to be prioritized differently. Commandalena is still happy about showing, and I love to show. But his 2015 commitments in the breeding shed limit what we can do and where we can go. He has to be available on an "as needed" basis throughout the breeding season (which includes most of the show season). So this year can't be about me and what I want to do. I have to think about what's good for the business of breeding. Again, my personal goals have to reflect reality. It's a good lesson for the rest of my life!

Do more and become a better person. In all aspects of life, I believe that working within a realistic assessment of goals and honoring your personal and professional commitments makes you a better person. I like to think that my involvement with Commandalena and everyone who has been associated with him or who will be associated with him makes my world richer and aids my personal growth. This amazing experience hasn't been about the wins or the trophies. It's about all the lessons I've learned that will enhance my life and build opportunities for the future.

Lesson #3: You have to believe

Of all the lessons I've learned over the past two years of my life with horses, the greatest one is this: To BELIEVE.

When I bought Commandalena, no one else had wanted to believe in a 20-year-old stallion, despite all of his accomplishments. His dollar value declined, but still, no one saw enough worth in him to purchase him. When I looked at him, even in his photographs, I didn't see his age. In his eye, I saw light.

I took a chance and believed in him. He repaid me with the best ride of my life, one that we continue together. His value to me is priceless and he is irreplaceable. The best part? Others have seen his light and, like me, they believe in him. He deserves it.

What My Horse Teaches Me

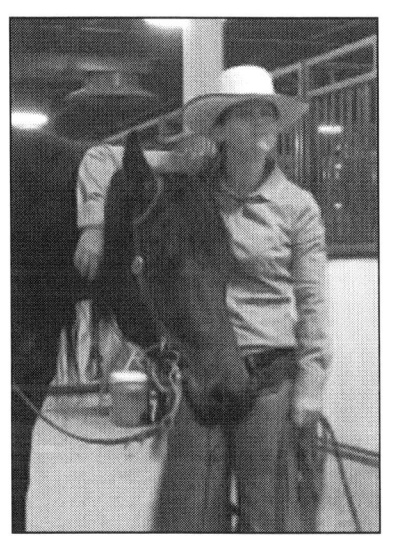

*Jessica Lea Gadd and Joan.
Photo courtesy of the author.*

WE ALL NEED SECOND CHANCES

By Jessica Lea Gadd

A lot of us go through life wanting a second chance—to be accepted, to be able to have unbreakable faith in another being, and to overcome challenges. My horse, Joan (I call her Joan for Joan Jett, but her registered name is Rock N Roll Red Pine) has given me those second chances—and transformed my life.

Joan came into my life about two years ago. I'd had horses on and off, as a child and as an adult. I made sure that my children had the opportunity to be with horses, despite the financial limitations of being a single parent. During the worst years of my life, I had to relocate for a job and ended up living in a new area where I knew no one. My only "friend" was my horse—a project and a puzzle that I couldn't solve. I had a long history as a good rider, but he was beyond my ability. I was afraid of him. I didn't have money for lessons or training and I worried about getting hurt. As much as I hated to do it, I sold him. He got a good home with people who could manage his issues.

But my failure to make things work with him hit me on many levels: I was totally alone. I felt as if I'd abandoned the horse that was my responsibility. For me, those feelings of being alone or let down by another person stretch as far as I can remember. I'm an only child. I never knew my father. The feeling that I'd given up on another being—knowing how badly it can hurt to be alone and to feel abandoned—burned my soul. I felt embarrassed, inadequate, and guilty because of the mistakes I thought I'd made with this horse.

My life eventually came together. I'm married to a wonderful man. I have great friends and terrific kids. But I still felt haunted by the past. I needed to give someone or something a second chance, and thereby give myself one, too.

Breaking the chain of abandonment

That's when Joan came into my life. I was looking for a horse that could restore my confidence and break my cycle of fear with horses. I'd also become interested in competing in the new ranch horse events. The first time I saw Joan, she stopped me in my tracks. She was the most beautiful horse I had ever seen. I saw so much potential in her. But I thought there was no way I could hope to own her.

I took lessons and studied techniques used by Ray Hunt and Buck Brannaman, who often says that it's the human, not the horse, who needs training. I thought about what I may have done wrong with the horse I gave away: Had I tried to force him to perform? Was I attentive enough to what he needed to be comfortable and willing? Had I made the right response to training easy and the wrong response difficult?

I tried to apply these concepts about horse training to every aspect of my life. I paid more attention to the people with whom I interacted. Rather than thinking primarily about what I wanted or needed, I tried to focus on what was going on with the other person and what I could do to help the process.

I kept looking for "my" horse. Joan was always in the back of my mind. She didn't have the life she deserved. She'd been started as a reiner but got behind through no fault of her own. Then she was fire-saled. At this point, she was not being ridden and spent all of her time in a heated barn, with just a little turnout each week in an indoor arena. It wasn't a good life for any horse. Every few months, I texted the owner "why don't you let me buy that horse?" She wasn't ready. Finally, I just made an offer—and it was accepted.

When we first walked out of the barn into snow and cold, I knew that Joan probably hadn't seen daylight in six months. She pranced, whinnied, and quickly showed me that she'd never been taught to get on a trailer. She'd probably been forced to do so, swatted by a helper armed with a broom until she jumped forward and into the enclosure.

On that blustery, icy day with no one to help me, I tried to teach her. I asked her to walk close to the trailer and then hoped that she'd step on. I opened the escape door so that it didn't look dark inside. I coaxed, I waited, I let her calm down and see that there was nothing to worry about… without much success.

I worked her in tight circles near the trailer and then let her stop at the trailer, so that the trailer became place to rest. It didn't work. She paid attention to everything except me, the trailer, and what I was asking her to do. It was as if she didn't want to acknowledge I was there. She tuned me out—and everything associated with me. I got the distinct impression that she had decided that there was no upside to working with people. She was like an office worker who sees nothing but a boring routine and does the absolute minimum. I realized that, to make her comfortable and happy, I had to get her to use her brain. I had to help her come alive again.

Restoring the "want to" in a damaged horse

Hours later, fingers numb and body exhausted, I called my trainer to come over and help me. She finally convinced Joan to walk into the trailer. We made it home. I wondered what else was in store for me. Quite a bit, as it happened: Under saddle, she carried herself with head out and body angled. She shook her head constantly. I called a chiropractor. Everything needed to be realigned. I checked her teeth: They were long and sharp. I called the dentist. Over time, her physical discomforts diminished, but she still was more interested in zoning out than in working with me.

Boredom, horses, and people

I asked myself: What makes me want to zone out and ignore everything around me? Boredom was high on my personal list, so I wondered if Joan might feel the same way. I focused on keeping her routine varied. If I felt her begin to zone out, I tried something new. I needed to work to keep her engaged and interested.

I also tried to avoid forcing her to do things. Instead, I tried to let her figure it out. I kept in mind the need to make the correct response easy and the incorrect one difficult for her. But I didn't insist. If she wanted to make things difficult, I let her—and hoped she'd eventually see that there was a better way to do things. More and more often, she did.

This way of thinking has carried over into other aspects of my life. For instance, at work, I may see someone making the same small mistake over and over. I used to pretty much order them to change the way they do things. Perhaps they would, but there'd be some resentment and the potential for zoning out.

These days, I'll offer help and advice. But I won't take things farther than that. Instead, I'll let them continue to make the mistakes (as long as these small errors don't affect the overall picture) and hope that they eventually decide to change their ways.

I do the same thing with my kids—as a mother, you want things done your way. But that's not always best for the long-term relationship. And in all things, I try to focus on the good, on my horse's accomplishments (or my children's or the people I work with), and I celebrate each small victory and improvement.

We started going to shows. I hoped that new environments and changes in routine would help her. And they did. I remember one class where I just barely had to ask for anything, and she gave her all for me. She had even more potential than I'd thought ... smart, talented, athletic... all she had needed was to get her "want to" back. She had needed to rediscover a desire to work—and try.

She's helped me, too. I'm proud that I didn't give up, that I worked through my problems with her. The feeling when we solve a problem is fantastic. It makes me want to do more, try harder, and I think she feels the same way.

When the horse helps the family

Joan has also brought my family closer together. I work second shift, which has always been a strain on everyone. Joan has made it easier—my husband and kids all want to chip in and care for her while I'm working. There's a sense of family and togetherness in this—of working and trying together.

In some ways, I think that, just as Joan zoned out around people, we often zone out around each other. Rather than do things together, we often will sit in front of a video game or a TV program. We're alone even when we're with other people. But that's no longer the way it is in my house: While I'm working, someone's always checking on Joan, feeding her, bringing her in and out of the barn, taking her blankets off, brushing her, petting her. They help me out a lot, and I know it's because they want to do it. Joan brings all of us closer together.

I never gave up on Joan—and that's given me a peace that I needed. I've learned to trust her, to ask for less, and never force her to do something. She's rewarded me by becoming an amazing kind and willing mare. In 2014, she proved how far she'd come. We won a host of state championships and national placings in Ranch Horse competition. This year, we'll add reining. I can't wait to see what other lessons I'll learn from this amazing horse!

LEAVING BROOKLYN

By Jodie Palella

Jodie Palella and Spike.
Photo: copyright © Jenny Johnson.

I grew up in Brooklyn, New York. And everything you hear about Brooklyn is true (at least in my neighborhood)—it's a place where people speak their minds, are impatient, and want things done right away. It's easy to think that your way is not only the best way but the only way to get things done. And this certainty carries over into all aspects of our lives, even after we grow up and leave home.

Learning how to fail and how to succeed

Brooklyn is also a loving and protective place to grow up. More than anything, my working-class parents tried to insulate me against risk for failure. For instance, my artistic mother always helped me with my school projects. Although my parents loved me dearly and meant well, the downside was that I was never allowed to fail.

That "I will not fail" and "I cannot fail" point of view became even more pronounced because so many things came easily to me. As a result, I became convinced that: 1) My way is the right way to do everything and 2) Failure is impossible.

It goes without saying that these beliefs may not be the best tools with which to overcome many of life's challenges. But I can say that my outlook—and how I respond to many situations—has changed quite a bit. I owe a lot of this to Spike, my quarter horse gelding.

He was a long time coming into my life. As a horse-crazy child, I saved my pennies and worked at a barn. As a teenager, I was able to buy my own horse and pay for his board. I took a break from horse activities during college, but once I could afford it, I bought two horses and lived my childhood dream. I boarded them at a nearby stable, learned western dressage, and finished my second year showing horses as grand and reserve champion in my discipline.

Then I decided that I wanted to try a new horse sport, reining. This event, based on working with cattle, features some high-powered maneuvers that look easy but they're not.

I ran right up against a wall that comes from being so sure that your way was the only way. It didn't work, and it set me up for the unthinkable—failure.

I struggled through months of trying to succeed with Spike. I learned important lessons that ended up transforming my life.

Here's what my horse taught me.

What My Horse Teaches Me

How to listen—and how to learn

Soon after I got Spike, I discovered that I was not only afraid to fail, but I was also afraid that I would make mistakes and mess him up. I convinced myself that I needed an instructor to tell me what to do at every step of the way if I was to avoid failure. In retrospect, I realize that—although I had felt very competent and successful in western dressage—I had become paralyzed in trying to solve problems with Spike. When things went wrong, I was at a total loss.

These issues were compounded by the fact that Spike was—by far—the most expensive horse I'd ever bought. He'd been professionally trained. I'd convinced myself that to succeed, I just needed to work harder to follow my instructor's directions: "Move your hand… now use your leg…now pick up your rein…" Over and over, I tried. And failed. And failed. And failed.

After the show season, which wasn't what I'd hoped for, I took Spike home for a winter break. There, riding on my own, I had a revelation: I been doing nothing more than going through the motions, mechanically following my trainer's directions.

What wasn't I doing? Listening to my horse, waiting for his response, and deciding what I should do next based on what my horse was telling me about what he felt, what he thought I was asking for, and what each of my signals was communicating to him. I had lapsed into my Brooklyn my-way-is-the-only-way frame of mind. That's when I had my "ah ha" moment and realized that, for so much of my life, I'd been insulated from failure. I hadn't really ever learned how to be comfortable making mistakes as I tried to solve problems. I hadn't learned the value of learning from my mistakes.

Now that I was working on my horse without a trainer's help, I reminded myself that I had years of experience with horses and that I could be on my own. Instead of using robot-cues to ask Spike to do one of the reining maneuvers, I thought back to when I was a teenager and rode for fun, without lessons, relying on my balance and my basics. I hadn't responded mechanically back then. I hadn't been determined to follow precise instructions yelled out by a trainer. Perhaps because I'd been riding for enjoyment and wasn't thinking about success or failure, I had been comfortable making mistakes. I had tried things, and I had fun.

The journey is the fun part

Learning to be comfortable with making mistakes changed my riding—and my life. My focus shifted from winning in the show ring to learning how to communicate with my horse. Soon, what interested me wasn't how many ribbons or trophies I might get, but the learning process itself. My takeaways:

- It didn't matter if I was always right.
- It didn't matter if my horse gave me the wrong response.
- What mattered was that we could learn from each other.
- To learn, we all need to make mistakes.
- It's better to wait and be patient than to "strong-arm your way through life."
- I need to appreciate our progress, not beat myself because I'm not perfect.

I found that this focus allowed me to take a step back and slow down in all aspects of my life—and actually embrace the failure when it happens—because I know I will learn from it.

This journey toward learning, understanding, and communicating also gave me so much happiness. I believe that my experience with Spike helped me deal with personal challenges that included the death of a family member and huge changes in my workplace (more on that later).

Something else happened… I'd had a decade of lower back pain, perhaps related to trying to physically force horses into doing what I want them to do (and mentally "muscling my way" through a lot of situations). All these problems cleared up.

I'm learning that, with horses and so much else in life, you first ask. Then you wait. And you trust that you'll get the right answer. If you don't, you figure out another way to get something done. But you can't force anyone (or any horse) to do what you want or give you the answer you'd like to hear.

Getting better results in my work and home life

About the time I got Spike—and started to focus on communication and realizing that my trainer's way wasn't the only way—huge staffing changes took place at work. People with different work styles and work histories came on board.

Fortunately, I was able to use the lessons I'd learned from my horse. I could step back and listen and think—as opposed to automatically react and "muscle my way" through in a "my way is the only way" mode. I'd become more receptive to other people's views and experiences.

This has allowed me to accept some good changes. I have been able to work with people who do not necessarily share my opinions or experience in terms of how to do specific tasks. I am more open to looking at how things might be done differently and achieve the same—or better—results.

Just as I want to work as a team with my horse, I am increasingly interested in working as part of a team with my coworkers. Spike has made me happier, kinder, more patient, and more forgiving. People—and horses—make mistakes. But that's no reason why you can't learn to work together!

This has also affected how I interact with my boyfriend. Just as I'm more interested in understanding other beings (horses and humans) and working to solve problems, I've become kinder at home. I've accepted that he'll make mistakes, I'll make mistakes, but we'll get through it together. There is no single "right" way, but a back-and-forth dialogue between the two of us.

I've been fortunate to own Spike and have this opportunity to learn. There's not much in our lives that helps us to stop and think about what we're really doing. The media and so much of our everyday routine encourage us to make knee-jerk reactions and snap judgments—and shoot our mouths off. Spike helps me listen to others and forgive—probably because he is so forgiving of my mistakes. I'm less critical of others and I feel that my experiences with him have helped me grow as a person.

When I think back on my life with Spike, I feel that I've grown and changed—all for the good—as a person, more than I would have thought possible. It feels great.

What My Horse Teaches Me

TRUST, KINDNESS, AND BECOMING MORE

By Sandy Corriveau

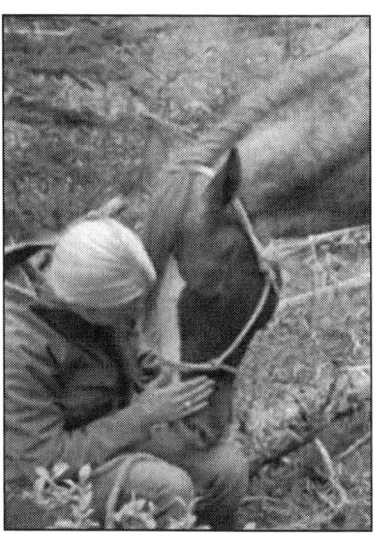

*Sandy Corriveau and Jagger.
Photo courtesy of the author.*

I never wanted to own a stallion, but five-year-old Jagger (Shiners Got Swagger) not only made me happy to have one in the barn but also gave me a new understanding of horses—what they think, what they feel, how to communicate with them, and how much joy they bring to my life. Because of him, I've learned to focus my training on building a horse's confidence. I apply many of those objectives to the rest of my life, particularly how I teach my children.

I have a lifetime of experience with horses. My dad taught me to ride before I could walk. His methods were old school: He would buy a cheap horse at an auction, throw a curb bit on it, and ride the buck out, without finesse. I followed in his footsteps, always with the nagging feeling that there might be a better way. Like my dad, I was always the boss when I worked with horses. After he died, the horses passed to me. I continued to work with them in the only way I knew how.

It wasn't until Jagger came along that I realized you can ride like the wind but still not know what you're doing—that's when I set out on a journey to better understand and communicate with my horse. I learned so much in the process.

Jagger came into my life when I bought his pregnant dam, Oaks Little Diamonds, in a sale. From the moment he hit the ground, he was special, with a mentality more akin to a kind and people-oriented puppy dog than a fractious colt vying for dominance. He never tried to kick or bite. He wanted to be with people. He's like that today: He's so gentle that I have to keep in mind that he is a stallion. More than once, someone has parked a mare right next to him—not even thinking that he might be a anything other than a broke gelding—and I've had to either move him or ask them to move. I don't want to set him up for misbehavior and failure.

In addition to his kindness, he has an amazing amount of try—so much that I feel that I need to be careful not to ask him to do too much and possibly hurt him or take the desire to work out of him. I want to learn as much as I can about training and showing so that everything in his life can be as good as possible. Enhancing my education is particularly important, as I now do almost all of his training by myself, just taking lessons when I can.

Believing in my horse

Even before he was ready for training, I was convinced that Jagger was special. I questioned my ability to get him started without messing him up. So I sent him to a trainer. After a few months, I got a call that he was showing too much undesirable stallion behavior and looking for a fight. In a situation like this, you have two options: 1) side with the trainer and let him address it or 2) believe in your horse and all that you saw in him from the day he was born. I decided that I believed in my horse more than the trainer. I brought Jagger home. I've always been glad I did.

In retrospect, I think the trainer might have pushed Jagger to the point that he rebelled and actually invited misbehavior. We've all seen horses that have been pushed to their wit's end and buck, kick, ignore the rider, or simply refuse to perform. We've all seen horses in training "factories" that produce performance-ready horses on a time line. If one gets injured, there are plenty more waiting in the wings. Jagger deserved more than that.

Over our five years together, he has inspired me to be a better rider, a better horseperson, and a better person. I spent a long time on the basics, and kept his routine varied, with everything from long trail rides and work on trail obstacles to work on cattle. I am careful to reward him for what he does right, even if it's just a simple "give" in response to rein pressure. I believe that Jagger respects me, as he would a dominant horse. He's never challenged my authority. Occasionally, I do have to get after him for something, but the lesson is quickly learned and we move on.

My approach with Jagger has also paid off in my work with Ava, my two-year-old filly. I focused on getting a good foundation, consisting of groundwork and very basic work under saddle to build confidence and basic skills. I didn't care how long the process took. I enjoyed every minute of it as I watched her blossom. She, like Jagger, tries so hard and wants to please.

Horses and children: So much alike

Ava and Jagger are completely different, both in their personalities and how they learn... but that's similar to the issues I face with my children, each so unlike the other. Both are, however, caring and good individuals who treat others with respect.

If I had to name one quality that I want to develop in both my kids and my horses it's to build a nurturing personality and framework for the future. I want to help them grow and try to become more. To let them go in whatever direction seems best for them. To be sure they have the confidence to try and fail and try again and eventually succeed.

As I think back on my life with horses, what I've learned from Jagger and Ava jumps out at me even more. Training a horse, like everything in life, takes confidence. We've all been told—in so many situations—what we can't do. We're told that we need to leave training to the professionals. But with Jagger, and later with Ava, I set out to learn what I needed to know. I worked to build my skills so that I could do the work on my own. I not only gave them confidence—I gave myself confidence as well.

Jagger is a reflection of my heart. He might end up being a great performance horse; he might not. I'll find happiness in the journey. This year, I'm breeding him to a few of my mares, all producers or money earners. I hope he passes on all of his wonderful qualities. But most of all, I want to continue my journey with the next generation—to explore what we can learn and how we can all grow—with joy.

*Stacey Stephens and Peptos Rock Star.
Photo: copyright © Joe Moliken.*

THE LIFE-LONG EFFECTS OF LIFE WITH HORSES

By Stacey Stephens

Horses have been part of my life for more than 20 years. They've taught me about joy, achievement, pain, and loss—all the aspects of our lives that enable us to grow as individuals, expand our awareness of the world around us, and allow us to explore new challenges and dreams. I am blessed to have them in my world.

Although each horse that passes through my life is special, a few individuals have literally changed my world and taught me amazing lessons. They include:

Scootin' Glory. She was my first horse, and she taught me heartbreaking lessons about loss when she died during foaling, leaving an orphan foal behind.

Scootin' Star (registered name Slidin Tothe Stars). This filly, the daughter of Scootin' Glory, came into the world too early, immediately lost her mother, and required full-time attention just to stay alive. She taught me about responsibility in a setting that had life-and-death implications—and in which I played a key role in determining the outcome.

Breezy Town. This incredibly intelligent horse could outsmart the best of us. She taught me about the importance of respect in dealing with other beings. If you respect the individual (horse or human), they will reward you by giving you the best they have to offer. This lesson affects every aspect of my life with horses (and people).

A Dimension in Time. She represents my passion for horses. Bred to be my western pleasure show horse, we never succeeded in that endeavor. Regardless, she remained with me during many very challenging times and serves as a shining representation of my ever-present love for these animals.

Peptos Rockstar. This wonderful horse taught me what patience and kindness are all about. He was my partner at the very beginning of my career in reining and caused me to fall in love with the sport. Among our most amazing experiences? The day when I, an overzealous beginner, attempted a sliding stop. I lost my position and ended up "riding his neck." As I got back in the saddle where I belonged, he turned his head to look at me with his kind eye, as if to say "What are you doing up there?" So many horses would have lost their ever-loving minds in this situation. I also had the unforgettable experience of riding him to a 70 (a reining score that indicates that all maneuvers were done correctly) the first time I showed in this sport. He literally carried me to this accomplishment. It was quite a while before I achieved this level of success again.

Hollywood Reminic. He is my "horse" soulmate. The connection to him—his kindness, generosity, and talent—inspires me to become a better rider, showman, and owner.

Choclatnmypnutbutr. This three-year-old colt is a dream come true. When I watch him perform, I sometimes think about how much I have learned though my years in the horse industry and how all that hard-earned knowledge culminated in my ability to see his potential—and led to my decision to select him as a prospect for the future.

I could go on and on about this long and wonderful journey. Over the years, I have participated in the American Quarter Horse Association, the American Paint Horse Association, the Palomino Horse Breeders Association, the American Pinto Horse Association, and the National Reining Horse Association.

I have had the opportunity to see the ebb and flow of the industry from the perspective of a ranch manager, breeder, and exhibitor. I have not only contributed personally, but I have also introduced the horse world to others who have become even more involved than I am. All of this has advanced both my personal growth and my strong sense of ethics and my skills in business.

I would not be who I am today without my horses.

What My Horse Teaches Me

Linda Carpenter and Peptos Rock Star.
photo: copyright © Joe Moliken.

FOR THE LOVE OF A HORSE

By Linda Carpenter

"Mom, when you get your horse..." those words changed my life forever. My love for horses began when my daughter, Stacey, announced that she intended to buy a horse. It continued to develop as soon as I met her mare, Scootin' Glory (also known as Mama Scooter). It was tested the following year, when Mama Scooter's foal was born weeks before the due date at a boarding facility with only run-in sheds. All night long, in the mud and rain, we struggled to assure the safety of both mare and foal. Unfortunately, Mama Scooter died soon after, before the baby even had a chance to nurse.

Around the clock labors of love

We were novice horse owners, facing the challenge of raising a newborn orphan foal. Baby Scooter spent her first five days and nights in an equine surgery suite. It was the only accommodation available that would keep her out of the rain. We then moved her to the garage of my townhouse and began a long vigil. For the next few weeks, my daughter and I took shifts, so that someone was always with the little filly—day and night—bottle-feeding and keeping her warm and healthy. As she became stronger, she also became noisier and more energetic. It was time to leave the garage. We moved her to a private stable. She had a stall. We spent each night in the breezeway.

A few weeks later, Baby Scooter was strong enough to stay alone for a few hours at a time. My daughter and I returned to our jobs, but we still checked on Baby Scooter during our breaks and at lunch. And we slept in the stable every night. I fell in love with this little filly. We named her Slidin Tothe Stars.

Growing my dream

Two years later, as a birthday gift, my daughter gave me the ultimate present—Scooter officially became mine. Realizing my love for this horse, I purchased property and started growing my dream… Paint My Quarter Ranch.

Scooter, with her history as an orphan raised solely by humans, presented a challenge when she started training, but she made it through limited reining and roping. She then retired to become the best mama horse in existence. She not only raised 10 babies of her own, but she also took orphans to nurse alongside them.

We still own three of her progeny, all accomplished performance horses. Slidin Time ("Skylar") is a champion rope horse. Reminis ("Hollywood") and Hollywood Reminic ("Tanner") show successfully in reining

When my breeding business slowed, Stacey and I started riding reiners. Now, as novice competitors, we face an entirely new and exciting set of challenges. We're progressing nicely, thanks to the training, coaching, and guidance of our trainer, Daniel Hoerauf, of Nova Reiners in Goldvein, Virginia.

After many years in the horse industry, I am now having the best time of my life.

What My Horse Teaches Me

*Katie Elkins and TJ.
Photo courtesy of the author.*

A PLACE TO HEAL

By Katie Elkins

I would love to begin this note with a brilliant insight, quote, or witty saying that sums up the connection I feel with the world because of the friendship I long ago found in horses. But that would not accurately convey the reality—and would almost be a betrayal—of this most complex, fragile, and sincere relationship that acts as a constant in my life. Often, my connection with horses feels like the banks of a river that guide me downstream on a journey of self-discovery. On that journey, I have overflowed with grief: I lost my father abruptly when I was 17 and then lost so many other relatives and friends who meant so much to me.

When the tears run dry

Always, when the tears run dry, and I need to find myself, the only place I've ever been able to grow from tragedy—the good way, the way we are supposed to—has been in the many late nights spent at the barn.

I learned early in my life that horses often know us better than we know ourselves. You can passively deny truths or ugliness about yourself. But you cannot lie about yourself to a horse. Yet some of the faults that repel most horses seem to attract certain others. Horses are every bit as complex as people. Some are followers and some are leaders. Some need to be coddled; some like you to be direct. Some need to learn the hard way. Some pay much more attention than you would ever have thought possible and all they need is the confidence to shine. The list goes on. But both horses and humans share a need for love, whether or not it is earned, warranted, or deserved.

I believe that my sincere need to understand these creatures and my obsession to find a clear common ground with them have helped me learn how to have a positive impact on the lives of other beings.

Horses have taught me that, if you proceed with grace and love in your interactions with others, you are more likely to succeed in your efforts to form a connection.

They have helped me see that choosing to give love and kindness—without expectations of reciprocity—has an earth-moving power all its own.

Tammy Mercer and Moroko. Photo courtesy of the author.

HOW MY HORSE GOT ME THROUGH MY TEENAGE YEARS

By Tammy Mercer

I'm not sure when I became aware that I needed a horse in my life, but the 2-year-old colt that I eventually ended up with made it possible for me to navigate a tough adolescence that included a poor self-image and friends who turned to drugs. The lessons I learned about caring for my horse and being responsible for him helped me become a productive adult. I believe that I knew—from a very early age—that having a horse in my life was the one thing I needed to get through my life.

How did it all start? My parents told this story over and over.

"I want a horse," I apparently announced as a toddler during my first encounter with a department store Santa.

"Well I don't know about that dear," he replied.

"Well how about a pony instead, Santa?"

Growing up, my siblings and all the neighborhood kids played "horse," galloping through backyards, leaping over benches, kicking up our heels, and neighing for all to hear. I read every library book about horses and horse care. My copy of *Black Beauty* was so well used that I could recite almost every word. The first sentence still tumbles easily off my lips: "The first place that I can well remember was a large pleasant meadow with a pond of clear water in it."

I never outgrew my passion, which I believe was embedded in my DNA. My soul cried out for the spirit of the horse; nothing would stop me achieving the ultimate goal: A horse of my own.

"If you want a horse, you'll have to save up for it yourself." Every conversation with my parents seemed to end with this declaration. We lived in a 1950s subdivision. Part of a middle-class two-income family, I was a first-generation "latch-key kid" who wore the house key on a string around my neck. A horse was a wild dream.

Hanging on to my dream

At the age of 11, I began to make my dream a reality. My father took me to the bank and I proudly deposited my first babysitting money, a whopping $2.50, into my horse fund. Every cent I earned for the next four years went into that account.

In high school, I was awkward and had little self-confidence. I withdrew socially. I became "uncool" to long-term friends and struggled to find a way to fit in. My grades plummeted. Although I was naturally athletic, my commitments to babysitting (and my horse funds) limited opportunities for sports participation. My mother's alcohol and prescription drug abuse, characterized by erratic behavior and regular shouting matches between my parents, added to my misery. Looking back, I can say this was my first foray into depression.

As my home life spiraled out of control, I never lost hope that one day I would have a special horse. Six months before my 15th birthday it happened. My father had a casual conversation with a co-worker about his horse-crazed daughter—and that led to an offer of a horse for $100.00.

That evening my father told me about the possibility, which depended on whether I liked the horse. Like the horse? I knew I would love my horse! And I did. Shasta was a lanky 16-hand, 2-year-old Quarter Horse/Saddlebred colt. When we met, he greeted me with a soft nicker and a gentle nuzzle from his velvet nose. I was smitten. I was sure he would be my special horse. He would be my best friend and my confidant. He would carry me into adulthood.

Horse training—how hard can it be?

Shasta had been trained to halter and lead. That was it. I figured the rest of training had to be easy, particularly because I'd learned so much by reading.

With a book in one hand and a lunge line in the other, Shasta and I embarked on our training journey. I spent countless hours on the ground, walking, talking to, and brushing Shasta. I even taught him to count! I led him along the roadways, over bridges and into water, preparing for our first ride. When that day came, it was as uneventful as one could imagine. Using the words I had used hundreds of times on the end of a lunge line, I gave the cues for "walk," "trot," and "canter," and with effortless ease Shasta transitioned into a riding horse.

My father was our financial backer. Each month he fronted the cost for board, shoes, grain, and hay. I put every cent I earned towards that debt. After six months, the little Keystone binder showed a few dollars on the positive side of the balance sheet. I took my first real job as a waitress at the local Big Scoop Restaurant. Eventually, I paid all of Shasta's expenses myself.

The horse that changed my life

I became more confident and gained friends. For my 16th birthday, my best human friend hosted a surprise party for me at the barn.

My relationship with Shasta lasted 13 years. He endured the many tears that flowed into his mane as this lost teenager tried to find herself in the world. Over time, I discovered that the "horsey set" accepted me; they encouraged my natural leadership style. Shasta became a natural as well. He could do almost anything, from leading trail rides, to barrel racing, participating in parades, or winning first place in local horse shows.

I grew up during the psychedelic 70s. My friends experimented with drugs. I've often said that the reason I never got involved with drugs was Shasta. I could purchase four bags of grain for what I would spend on pot or pills.

In my mid-20s, despite my best efforts, I knew that I could no longer afford the "luxury" of owning a horse while living in a major city on a meager clerical salary. I could not manage Shasta's ever increasing boarding costs, and my rent, food, and transportation. Sadly I had to make the very difficult decision to re-home Shasta. I settled on a 14-year-old girl who was beginning her journey with horses. Shasta would become this girl's friend and confidant, as he had been mine.

I bravely smiled as I loaded Shasta into the horse trailer for the last time. I said goodbye to my friend with a final pat and a kiss on his velvet black nose. As the trailer disappeared down the gravel road, I cried so hard I thought my heart was breaking. Even though I knew I was making a good decision, and my Shasta was going to a fantastic home, I felt like I had let him down. He was my very best friend; he had stood beside me through good times and bad. He had carried me through my teenage years, where confusion and hurt were everyday occurrences. He had brought me to young adulthood. He had been the one I told all my "firsts" to: my first boyfriend, first car, first job… What would I do without him? I knew my life would never be whole until I had a horse again. It was then I vowed that one day I would make that happen.

I did, some 20 years later, but that's a whole other story!

What My Horse Teaches Me

What My Horse Teaches Me

Photo courtesy of the author.

A RUNAWAY HORSE, A PRESSURE WASHER, AND A LESSON FOR THE FUTURE

By Valerie Hicks

At age 15, I learned the ultimate lesson in humility from a buckskin quarter horse. I reflect on this episode every time I think I might be getting a little too full of myself.

In those days, I was, with help from my mom, training horses for some of our neighbors. This meant that not only was I doing something I loved, but—because I had a job—I was also able to get out of doing the crack-of-dawn chores on our dairy farm.

It was a lot of work; in the summer, I rode 10 horses a day. One of them was the infamous lesson-teaching buckskin. She had a lot of scars—the physical ones that crisscrossed her legs, a result of being tangled in a barb wire fence, as well as the emotional scars that accompany such an injury. She was terrified of ropes and confinement. But she was a big, powerful horse with a big heart and a lot of try.

Before long, I had her working well for me. When she allowed me to put a rope all down her scarred legs, I felt we had made a big breakthrough.

Like any horse-crazy teenager, I was so excited about my accomplishments that I just had to show someone.

How wrong can things go?

I led the mare over to the barn where my parents were hard at work milking cows. I sneaked up as close to the door as I could, hoping to snag someone's attention. I failed to notice the nearby pressure washer, on loan from a neighbor. Its long hose lay coiled on the ground. As I walked forward, the mare accidentally placed her foot—perfectly centered—inside a loop of hose. Carefully, I tried to step her out of the loop. She moved her foot just enough to make the loop curl around—and touch—her pastern. At that point everything seemed to shift into slow motion.

She panicked, remembering her past leg injuries. As she jumped backward, the hose tightened even more. She pulled the lead rope out of my hand. Just as my parents walked out of the barn to see what I'd accomplished, she wheeled around and tore off down the driveway—with the pressure-washer hose twirling in the air and the big machine bouncing behind her, parts flying off as if in a crazy TV cartoon.

In an instant, all my pride and joy were replaced with a great humility and shame. I had known better. I shouldn't have been there. I learned in that one instant not to be too proud. I don't think I ever rushed to gloat over my accomplishments after that—at least not any time during that summer. And yes, I spent the next few months paying for a very broken pressure washer.

What My Horse Teaches Me

*Gianna Marie Pickett and Forrest.
Photo: copyright © Image Hounds.*

THROUGH MY GRANDDAUGHTER'S EYES

By Gianna Marie Pickett
with Dee Hertig

My granddaughter, Gianna Marie Pickett, loves nothing better than to ride her paint horse. We call him "Forrest," named for Forrest Gump. You know the line, "Run, Forrest Run?" Well, that's what we call out to this great little horse. The only problem is, no matter how enthusiastically we urge him on, Forrest is the laziest horse I've ever seen. He would never run, which makes him perfect for a five year old!

What has Forrest taught her? I went straight to the source and asked Gianna. She tells me that she has learned an awful lot about what Forrest needs: To be fed, have water, get groomed, and be loved.

"If I don't take care of Forrest," she pauses. Her expression tells me that what follows is going to be a very scary thought. "I won't be able to ride."

She knows that he needs new shoes more often than she does. She knows how to clean his stall, grabbing the pitchfork to show me how it's done.

As Gianna's grandmother, I'm certainly biased, but I'm very proud that she not only understands the importance of loving animals—but that she also understands the need to care for and respect them.

We talk some more about what she learns from Forrest. Here's what Gianna tells me.

Be patient. When Gianna clucks to Forrest and uses her little legs to get him to go forward, it doesn't always work. But Gianna tells me that she knows she can't get mad at him. She just shrugs and says she has to "do it again" and "do it again" and "do it again" until he does what she asks him to do. I love watching her work with him. When she finally does get him to "go," you should see her smile!

Analyze. Sometimes, when Gianna rides Forrest, he tries to head over to the grass and graze. I ask her why she thinks that happens. "He wants to," she tells me. And then we talk about how important it is for her to learn to feel the first sign of Forrest doing something she hasn't asked him to do. I can see the wheels turning and a lot of concentration as she thinks through the problem and what she'll need to do to fix it. I'm thrilled because I can see that she's learning to analyze and solve problems.

Be grateful. Gianna knows that her parents bought Forrest to help her learn how to ride—and that she should always say "thank you" when they (or anyone else) help her with Forrest. She very rarely forgets!

What My Horse Teaches Me

THINGS ALWAYS GET BETTER— EVENTUALLY

By Shelby Lukes

Shelby Lukes and Starlight. Photo courtesy of the author.

Whenever it looks like things can only get worse, they will always get better—eventually. That's the biggest lesson I've learned from horses. I've been riding since I was six. I'm now 10 years old.

I started with weekly lessons. Then my parents leased a pony for me. Finally, when I was seven and a half, I got a pony of my own—Starlight. I loved her, and we did pretty well as a team.

But my family and I were not very "horse smart" back then. Starlight probably had some pre-existing conditions we didn't know about. Plus, she was always suffering from sort of medical problem—pulled stifles, laminitis, a spider bite that almost killed her, and finally, a broken hip.

Each time something went wrong, we came back slowly and did even better than before. For instance, we had jumping issues for a while. We figured out that Starlight had a physical problem, so we stopped jumping. While she recovered, we did nothing but flat work for a whole summer. All that flat work fixed the jumping issues.

We both performed better, but as we did, the work got harder. Ultimately, it became too much for Starlight. I could see it in her attitude. She tried to stay willing, but we knew that she had to be in pain. We worked really hard for her to recover but the vet finally said she just wasn't ever going to be able to do much more than walk and a trot.

After all the work we'd done and setbacks we'd had, I was so sad that my partner wasn't going to be able to work with me any longer. We don't have the space to keep a pet pony at home, but we made a deal with Starlight when we bought her that she was family—you don't just toss family members aside when they're no longer useful. We were very lucky to find a barn that needed a good little pony to teach kids about ponies!

I quit riding—how could I do it anymore without my Starlight? But I really loved horses and found this sport called "reining" that I wanted to try.

Now, I have a horse named Nugget, a sport I love, and a new barn family. I still get to visit Starlight. It's fun to see that she's happy and that so many other kids get to love her, too. I traded hunters (which I didn't love but I sure do love Starlight) for something so much better.

You just have to remember that even if bad things are happening, good things will come from it.

What My Horse Teaches Me

LEARNING FROM THE PAIN

By Susan Whitehead

Susan Whithead and Whizzy. Photo courtesy of the author.

It's easy to forget how much other beings rely on us—those who can't speak with words but whose feelings, emotions, and intelligence touch our souls. I ask myself every day: Do I pay enough attention to make their lives the best they can be?

It breaks my heart whenever I feel that I may have inadvertently contributed to another being's physical or emotional suffering. But I try to learn from my mistakes, and those of others.

The biggest lesson I learned took place nine years ago, and it haunts me to this day. I bought my horse Whizzy from a well-known trainer in Texas. I was told that the little gelding had previously had a condition called equine protozoal myeloencephalitis, which can have devastating and sometimes irreversible effects that limit a horse's athletic ability. When I watched a sale video, I saw no signs of the disease, which generally makes a horse look uncoordinated. The trainer told me that he was "free and clear" of the condition.

On film, he was gorgeous, with a long, flowing mane and all the athleticism you could ask for. But when he stepped off the trailer, I saw just a mousy, tiny sorrel horse. When I rode him, he was fine when he circled or performed his maneuvers to the left—but not to the right. My first reaction was that I had to be doing something wrong.

Trainers labeled him bad-minded and uncooperative. I was certain that the extreme differences between how he performed when traveling to the right versus the left had to mean something more. There just had to be a physical component. I was more convinced that his issues were physical when I learned that he often sat dog-like in his stall.

Putting the horse first

I did everything I could, to no avail. A lot of people said I should just get rid of him and move on. I couldn't. More than anything, I wanted him to be comfortable. So he spent his final years turned out in a 20-acre pasture. He loved to be around people and, despite his extreme problems when asked to travel to the right, he really did seem to love to be ridden and to work. Occasionally, I jumped on him bareback. I was careful to only do what he enjoyed and was physically and mentally comfortable with doing.

Whizzy taught me to always put the animal—the being without a voice—first. I learned to look first for physical issues and discomfort that may affect behavior. I learned to be more observant in my interactions with animals. I learned that just because you can't find a physical problem doesn't mean it's not there.

And I learned to treasure each moment I spend with horses.

What My Horse Teaches Me

What My Horse Teaches Me

ABOUT THE AUTHORS

Linda Carpenter, a retired Registered Diagnostic Medical Sonographer at St. Jude Medical Center in Fullerton, California, lives in Broad Run, Virginia, with her daughter, Stacey Stephens, and son-in-law, Steve Stephens. She rides reining horses under the guidance of Daniel Hoerauf of Nova Reiners and owns Reining in Color Farm, standing the stallion Hollywood Reminic, a son of Reminic N Dunit.

Claire Chisolm lives in Fayetteville, Pennsylvania, with her husband and Maizy, her amazing rescue dog. She teaches her own style of fun, mindful yoga and hula hooping in the Chambersburg, Pennsylvania, area. She has two grown daughters and two grandsons. She is still on the lookout for her next great teacher.

Sandy Corriveau lives near Red Deer, Alberta, Canada, with her husband and two children. She is a stay-at-home mom who takes care of her family, trains her horses, and cares for other animals, including chickens, dogs, and cats.

Kim Duckworth lives in Dalton, Pennsylvania, with her little girl, Katharine, and four horses. She is the owner/teacher of Endless Mountains Hot Yoga studio.

Katie Elkins teaches riders of all ages at Kaytee Reiners and Performance horses in Doswell, Virginia. A former assistant trainer to a number of internationally known horse trainers, she also competes locally and regionally.

Jessica Lea Gadd is married with three sons, one grandson, and one granddaughter. The household also includes three pet dogs and several coon hunting dogs used by her husband and boys for hunting, and, of course, one horse—Joan. Jessica works in a hospital dietary department. She enjoys small-town country life and close friends.

Samantha Gothe and her husband Vic Gothe live on 125 acres in Kennerdell, Pennsylvania. She works as a hair stylist. Her only child is the Aussie Kya.

Dana Grafft lives in Germantown, Maryland, with her husband. A compliance expert in the pharmaceutical industry, she also owns and stands the stallion Commandalena, with lifetime earnings in excess of $143,000, and competes in reining.

Valerie Hicks earned an Associate Degree in Horse Management and a Bachelor Degree in Animal Science. Activities with miniature horse, pony, and donkey rescue fill her free time and even involves her non-horsey husband. To earn enough for her equines' keep, she operates a print shop.

Tina Lucas lives in Hanover, Virginia, with her husband Mike and daughter Sophie. She is a nurse practitioner at a busy level-one trauma center. The stress of caring for others is incredibly exhausting; her horses help her find balance and a sense of calm. She shares her love of horses with her daughter. The two of them can often be found together at horse shows and equine events.

Shelby Lukes is a seventh grade homeschooler with a passion for horses, dogs, building things, and playing her clarinet. She took her first riding lesson after turning six years old and hasn't looked back. She's done hunters, jumpers, western speed, and trail. She currently competes in reining. When she isn't riding her horse Nugget, she is building riding rings and barns and designing blankets, boots, and tack for her enormous Breyer horse collection. She lives with her family, two dogs, pony, horse, and various foster dogs in Northern Virginia.

Amanda McKinney of Chesapeake, Virginia, is a stage manager and local animal advocate who has transported hundreds of animals to spay/neuter surgeries and delivered doghouses and straw to many cold, lonely outside dogs. In addition to her rescued Tennessee Walking Horses, Rocky Top and Skywalker, Amanda and her husband Nathan share their home with five dogs: Louie, Cooper, Schuester, Junior, and Little Joe.

Tammy Mercer is a lover of horses and dogs—well, really all animals. She lives on five acres near Fanny Bay, a small community on Vancouver Island off the coast of British Columbia, Canada. She and her partner Keir have four horses, three dogs, and one cat. Their partnership Riding For Freedom Ranch Ventures serves as the umbrella company for an assortment of enterprises and horse-related products.

Jodie Palella lives in Howell, New Jersey, with two of her three quarter horses, Hallmark and Cisco. She is looking forward to the journey with her newest horse, Spike.

Wendy Peterson lives in New Market, Maryland. She is proud to have been a stay-at-home mom of two but now that the children are venturing off to college, she finds herself back in her original field of insurance (including equine) as well as a brand partner for Nerium International. Her hobbies include competitive horse showing, gardening, and reading. Her furry child Bandit, an Australian Shepherd, goes wherever possible with her. She is a member of the American Quarter Horse Association and the National Reining Horse Association.

Gianna Marie Pickett resides in North Texas with her reining parents Andrew and Sabrina Pickett. At five years old, she will graduate from pre-school May 2015. She has been known to wear a tutu over her jeans. She is learning to ride on her reining horse Mark Me (nicknamed Forrest) under the guidance of her parents. Gia has already conquered lead line classes and will soon show in short-stirrup reining. Gia's grandparents are long-time reiners Jack and Dee Hertig and Nancy Johnson of Aubrey and the late Ed Pickett, who built and ran Green Valley Farm in Aubrey, Texas.

Elizabeth Pino lives in central Massachusetts with her husband and their Belgian Malinois, Marlee, and her amazing quarter horse Chexys Lady In Red (aka "Moey") who is transitioning from a successful reining career to a promising second career in dressage. She is the proud aunt of a talented niece and two gifted nephews. She works for an American multinational technology and consulting corporation.

Kim Croom Smith lives in Wrightsville Beach, North Carolina. She is a registered nurse by trade but currently is a full-time mom to three awesome boys, Cameron, 19; Breeze, 13; and Bowan, 12. Her husband Ben is a dentist and a marlin fish chaser. A nonhorseman, he will occasionally go to shows and clap "once in a while" for her. She is now 54 years old and her doctors continue to be astonished that she is able to do what she does. She is indeed free, thanks to the Lord first and to Moses second.

Stacey Stephens lives in Broad Run, Virginia, with her husband Steve Stephens, mother Linda Carpenter, and various pets. She works for Innovatient Solutions Inc., a software firm specializing in interactive patient care. When she is not working, she rides reining horses under the guidance of Daniel Hoerauf of Nova Reiners and acts as the breeding manager for Reining in Color Farm. Reining in Color specializes in well-bred Paint reining horses.

Susan Whitehead, of Millville, New Jersey, has been following the reining industry since the National Reining Horse Association was founded in the late 1960s, although she only competed for the few years that she owned Whizzy. The pair showed in the green reiner (beginner) division. After many years, she still misses her horse.

Amy Wiggs lives in Windsor, Virginia, with her husband Dave and three stepchildren, one with cerebral palsy. She is a service administrator for a national boiler company and works at the farm where she boards her horses. She also volunteers for Diamonds In The Rough, a local equine rescue.

Sandy Wood lives in Florida, New York, with her husband John. She is an elementary school principal for the Warwick Valley Central School District in Warwick, New York. Rock shares Sandy's heart with Lily Moo, a black and white Chihuahua, and Charlie, the cat!

Printed in Great Britain
by Amazon.co.uk, Ltd.,
Marston Gate.